100 QUESTIONS AND ANSWERS

EXPLORERS AND VOYAGES OF DISCOVERY

Written by
Margarette Lincoln

Edited by
Nicola Wright & Dee Turner

Designed by
David Anstey

Illustrated by
Mainline Design, Richard Draper & Peter Bull

PUFFIN BOOKS

Dr Margarette Lincoln is Assistant Head of Education at the National Maritime Museum, London. She has taught in schools and universities. Her publications include resource materials for teachers and several children's books.

PUFFIN BOOKS

Published by the Penguin Group
Penguin Books Ltd, 27 Wrights Lane, London W8 5TZ, England
Penguin Books USA Inc., 375 Hudson Street, New York, New York 10014, USA
Penguin Books Australia Ltd, Ringwood, Victoria, Australia
Penguin Books Canada Ltd, 10 Alcorn Avenue, Toronto, Ontario, Canada M4V 3B2
Penguin Books (NZ) Ltd, 182-190 Wairau Road, Auckland 10, New Zealand

Penguin Books Ltd, Registered Offices: Harmondsworth, Middlesex, England

First published 1993
10 9 8 7 6 5 4 3 2 1

Produced for Puffin Books by Zigzag Publishing Ltd, 5 High Street, Cuckfield, Sussex RH17 5EN
Series concept: Tony Potter
Design Manager: Kate Buxton
Cover illustration: Graham Humpreys

Colour separations by RCS Graphics Ltd, Leeds
Printed in Belgium

Contents

About this book

This book answers all your questions about people's exploration of the world from the earliest recorded times to the present day. It is packed full of fascinating facts about heroic journeys across unknown oceans, through hostile lands, into space and under the sea.

What were the earliest boats made from? Who first sailed around the world? Which explorers first saw kangaroos? What is a diving bell? What do astronauts eat? These are just some of the many questions you will find out the answers to.

Who were the first explorers?

To frighten off other travellers, the Phoenicians spread tales of sea serpents.

Phoenicians ruled the Mediterranean for 1000 years from 1400 BC.

The earliest explorers lived in prehistoric times, more than half a million years ago. They were Stone Age people in the land now called Africa, searching for new sources of food and shelter.

Q Why did people begin to explore?

A Exploration was often a question of survival. People hoped to find fresh supplies of food and living materials and often a safer place away from enemies.

Q How did people first explore?

A The first explorers probably travelled on foot or on horseback. But it was easier to travel greater distances across the sea or along rivers by boat.

Q Who were the greatest early explorers to cross oceans?

A The Phoenicians, who lived in what is now Israel, built a large fleet of ships around 800 BC. They travelled as far as Africa and the British Isles to trade.

Q What were the earliest boats made from?

A Boats might have been made from hollowed-out logs, reeds, or skins stretched over a wooden frame.

Q What cargoes did ships carry?

A Egyptian ships carried wood, ivory, silver, gold, cloth and spices. They also carried animals.

Q Who first sailed around Africa?

A The dangerous journey round what is now called the Cape of Good Hope was made by the Phoenicians in about 600 BC .

In about 1500 BC, Queen Hatshepsut of Egypt sent five ships to Punt (now called Somalia) for spices, monkeys, dogs and minerals.

Q Who was the most famous of the early explorers?

A Alexander the Great was a famous Greek general and explorer. He explored in order to conquer. By 326 BC his conquests stretched from Egypt in the West to northern India in the East.

How did early explorers find their way?

Viking sailors sometimes relied on the instinct of birds. From time to time they would release a raven and follow it, hoping it would lead them to land.

Before modern instruments such as radar and radio were invented, explorers had to use other methods to discover their position at sea and in strange lands.

About 3000 years ago, Polynesians were exploring the Pacific islands in canoes. To navigate they studied the positions of the stars, wind direction and the pattern of ocean waves.

Q How did the earliest explorers navigate?

A Navigators studied the position of the Moon, Sun and stars. Some also knew how to sail along a given latitude (distance north or south of a line called the Equator which runs round the middle of the Earth).

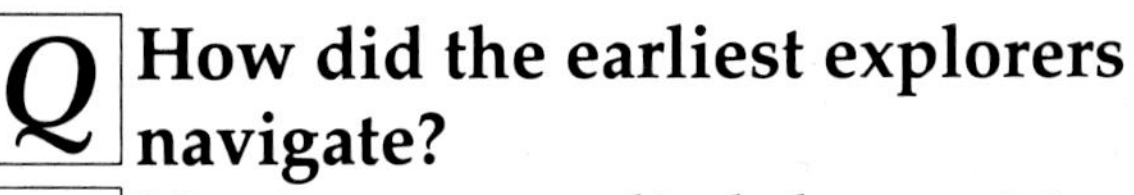

Q How did explorers find remote islands?

A Early sailors could guess where land lay from the behaviour of sea creatures and from the shape and size of waves. Their boats may have been carried across the ocean by currents.

Q How did sailors know they were near land if they didn't have a chart?

A Sailors knew they were near land when they saw birds or floating vegetation. Sometimes the colour of the sea or the shape of clouds changed near land.

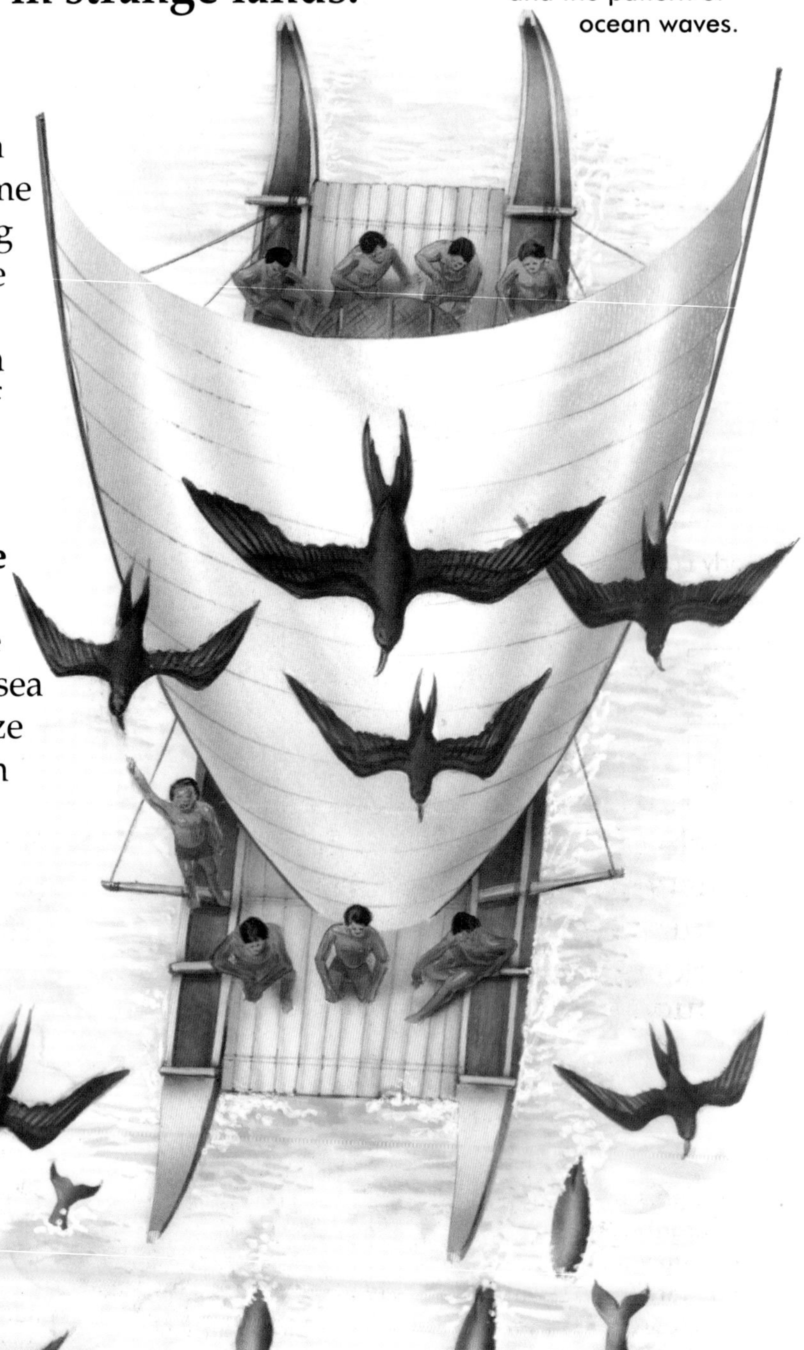

The telescope was invented in the early 17th century.

Q Who invented the compass?

A The Chinese invented the first compass about 4000 years ago. However, European explorers did not use them until about 1000 years ago.

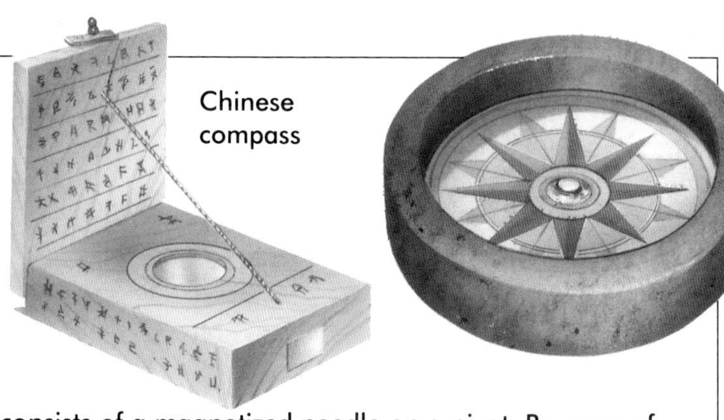

A compass consists of a magnetized needle on a pivot. Because of the Earth's magnetism, the needle always points to magnetic north.

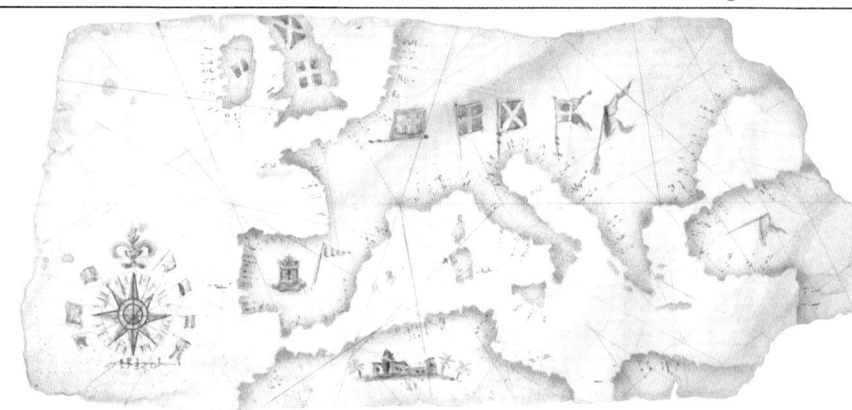

Early charts, called portulan charts, were drawn on stretched animal skin (parchment).

Q What were early charts like?

A In the 15th century, charts showed coastal features, ports and danger spots. Direction lines radiated out from compass points to help seamen follow a direct course from one place to another.

Q What was a quadrant used for?

A The quadrant was the earliest instrument used to measure the height of the Sun or stars. It was invented by the Arabs. In the 15th century, seamen used it to work out their latitude.

The sights of a quadrant were lined up with the Sun or a star. The plumb line showed the number of degrees above the horizon to work out a ship's position at sea.

Q What was an astrolabe?

A Like the quadrant, the astrolabe was used to work out latitude. Both instruments were fairly inaccurate at sea, when readings were taken on a rolling deck.

Astrolabes were made of brass. There were two holes at either end of the arm, which were lined up so the Sun or a star shone through. The arm then showed the height above the horizon.

How far did the Vikings travel?

Some Vikings dared to sail into the unknown Atlantic - to the Faroes, Iceland, Greenland and even America.

Longships were shallow in depth, so Vikings could sail a long way up rivers and estuaries.

The Viking Age began around AD 800 and lasted about 300 years. Vikings explored many distant lands including parts of Russia and North America.

Q Why did the Vikings search for new lands?

A Scandinavia, where the Vikings came from, has long, cold winters and much of the land is difficult to farm. Large families could not grow enough food, so new places to live had to be found.

Q Which was the first Viking colony?

A The Vikings first discovered Iceland in AD 860 when a group of explorers were blown off course. Irish monks had already reached the island about 65 years earlier.

Q What were Viking ships like?

A Vikings warships were known as longships. These were fast, sleek ships, well suited to raiding and long-distance travel.

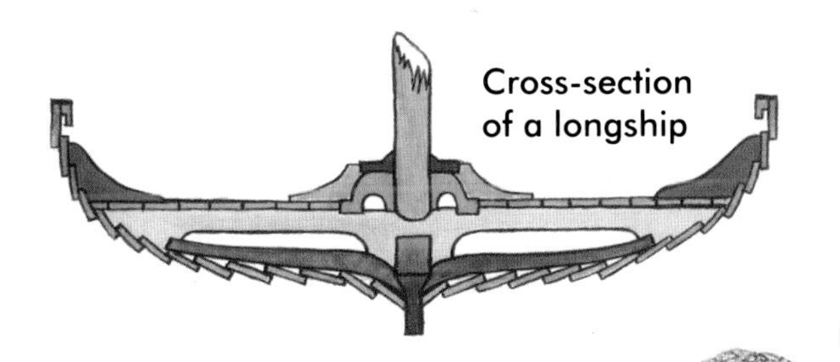

Q What goods did the Viking traders want?

A They wanted gold, silver, spices, silk, jewellery and iron.

Q Where did the Vikings go?

A The Vikings raided France, Britain and Ireland. They sailed around Spain and into the Mediterranean. Vikings journeyed down the great rivers of Russia to reach the Caspian Sea and the Black Sea. They also crossed the Atlantic to North America.

Q Where did the crew sleep?

A There were no cabins on Viking ships. Viking sailors just covered themselves with animal hides or blankets, though some ships had awnings (roof-coverings). Voyages were not normally made in the coldest winter months .

Q Where did Vikings put their cargo?

A Viking ships did not have decks. Cargo was stored on the floor in the middle of the ship between the oarsmen who sat in the bow and stern.

Knarrs were probably no more than 18m long.

On voyages Vikings ate smoked fish, dried meat and vegetables.

Q What were Viking cargo ships like?

A Vikings carried cargo in ships called knarrs, which were wider than longships and mostly used for coastal trading.

Arab merchants who traded with India and the Far East were incredibly rich.

Who were the first Arab explorers?

Arabs played an important part in the history of exploration. In the 6th and 7th centuries they conquered a huge empire, spreading education and their religion, Islam.

Q What sort of ships did Arabs have?

A Arab ships were known as dhows. They had triangular sails, and needed only a small crew.

Q Where did Arab explorers learn about navigation?

A Arabs learned about navigation in the Indian Ocean while on trading missions. They worked out how to find their way by the stars. They also learned about tides, ocean currents and the monsoon cycle (heavy rainstorms).

Q Did Arab explorers make maps?

A Yes. There is a famous map of about 1150 made on a silver tablet by an explorer called Idrisi. He was a Spanish-born Arab who visited France and England as well as the East.

Early maps included only the top of Africa. The ship-like figure on the left is meant to show three lakes feeding into the River Nile.

Q Who was the greatest Arab explorer?

A The most famous Arab explorer was Ibn Batuta from Tangier in North Africa. He visited many countries from 1325 to 1355.

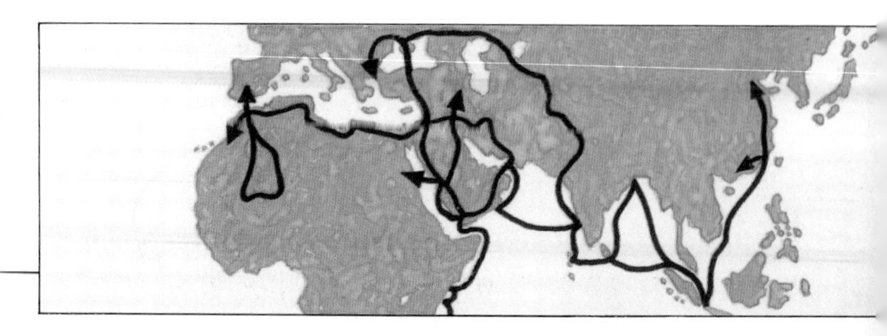

Stories about Arab merchants inspired many adventure stories, including Sinbad the Sailor and The Thousand and One Nights.

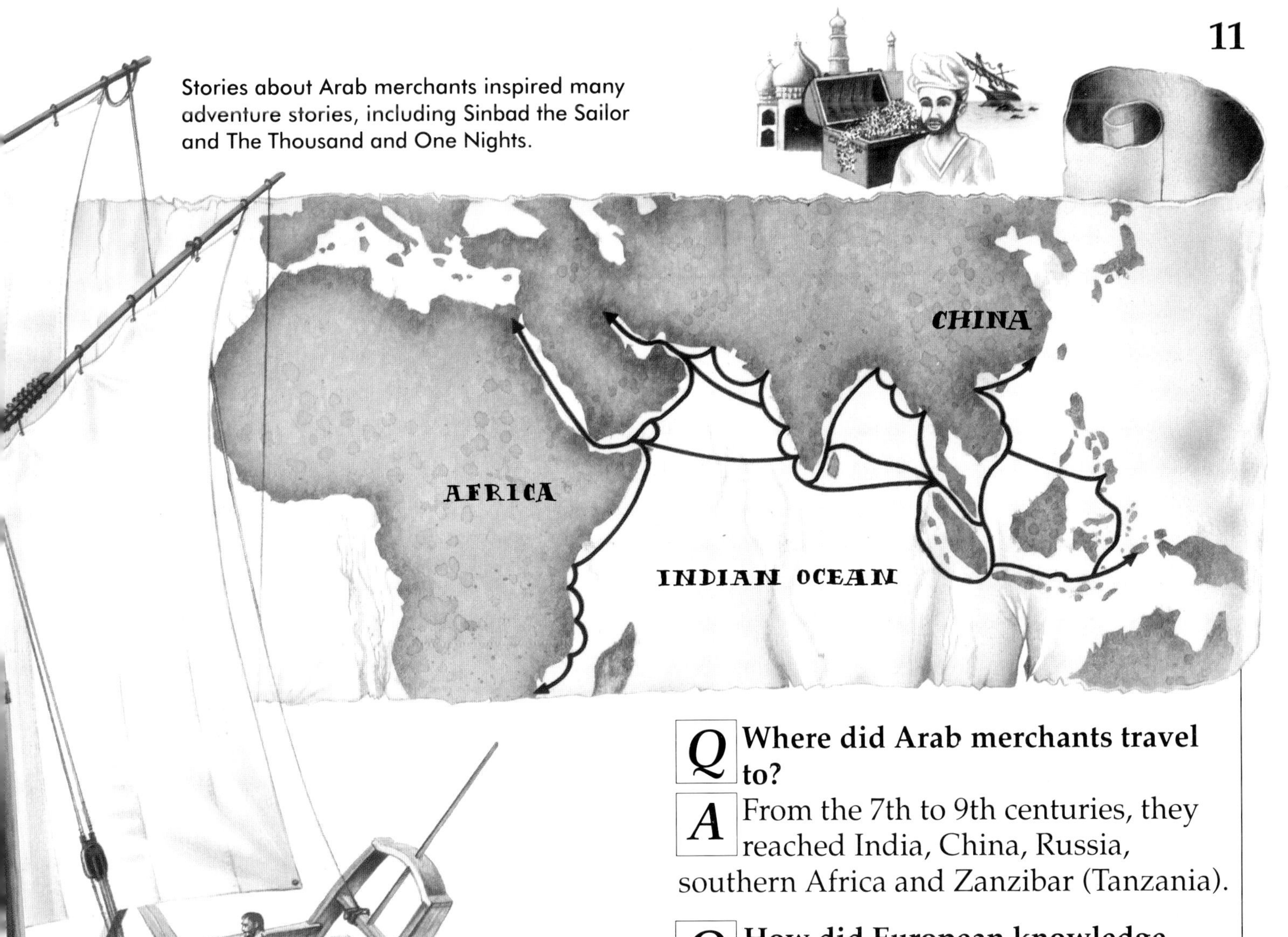

Dhows are still used in the Indian Ocean today.

Q Where did Arab merchants travel to?

A From the 7th to 9th centuries, they reached India, China, Russia, southern Africa and Zanzibar (Tanzania).

Q How did European knowledge compare with that of the Arabs?

A Europeans knew less about science, mathematics and geography than the Arabs. Their view of the world was restricted by Christian beliefs. On European maps the Earth was shown as a circle with Jerusalem at its centre.

India
Asia
China
Tower of Babel
Jerusalem
Europe
Africa

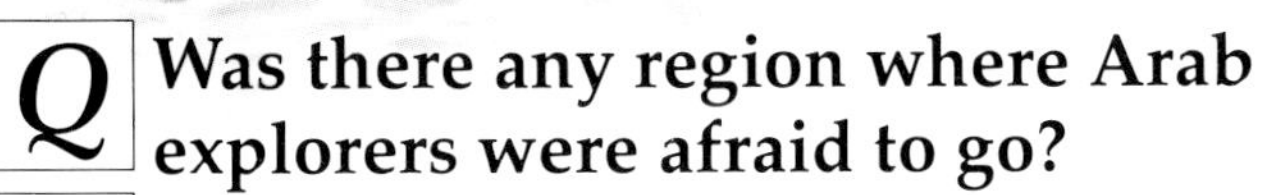

Q Was there any region where Arab explorers were afraid to go?

A Arabs called the Atlantic 'The Sea of Darkness'. Idrisi may have sailed into it, but if he did he was the only Arab who dared to do so.

Q How did the West come to share Arab learning?

A Christian knights came into contact with the Arabs during the Crusades (1096-1291) when the Christians tried to win back Jerusalem. Arabs had also conquered much of Spain.

Ibn Batuta travelled about 120,000km during his 30 years of voyages.

Who first made contact with China?

China, in the Far East, was a difficult place to reach. In 1271 Marco Polo, the son of a merchant from Venice, Italy, travelled overland to Peking (Beijing) with his father and uncle and spent many years with the Chinese emperor Kublai Khan.

Q What did merchants want from the Chinese?

A Western merchants wanted silk, spices and porcelain which they traded in return for gold and silver.

Q Why did Marco Polo travel to China?

A Marco's father, Niccolo, and his uncle, Maffeo, had already spent 15 years in China. They returned to Italy and then, in 1271, decided to go back, taking Marco with them. They carried gifts from Pope Gregory X, who hoped the great Mongol leader Kublai Khan would recognize Christianity as superior to the many other religions in China.

Q How long did Marco stay in the Khan's court?

A The Khan kept Marco at his court for 17 years, sending him on diplomatic missions all over China. Because of his quick grasp of languages and his skill at making notes on everything he saw, Marco was able to report back to Kublai Khan and, later, to people in Venice.

Q Were the Polo family the first Europeans to reach China?

A No. The route known as the Silk Road, which ran from China to the West, had been used by traders since about 500 BC, but the Polos were the first Europeans to travel its entire length and make contact with Chinese leaders.

Q How did the Polos travel to Shangdu, where Kublai Khan had his palace?

A They used camels to carry provisions through Armenia into Persia (Iran), through Afghanistan, the Gobi Desert and China. They travelled 11,200km, and took three and a half years to reach Shangdu. On the way they spent a year in Kanchow learning the customs of the Mongol peoples.

Junks were flat-bottomed ships with sails made of matting stiffened with wooden strips. They could make long voyages.

Q How did Marco return?

A Marco was given the job of escorting a princess to Persia (Iran), where she was to marry a prince. After stopping at Sumatra, Java, Malaya, Ceylon (Sri Lanka) and India, he delivered the princess to Persia and sailed home to Venice.

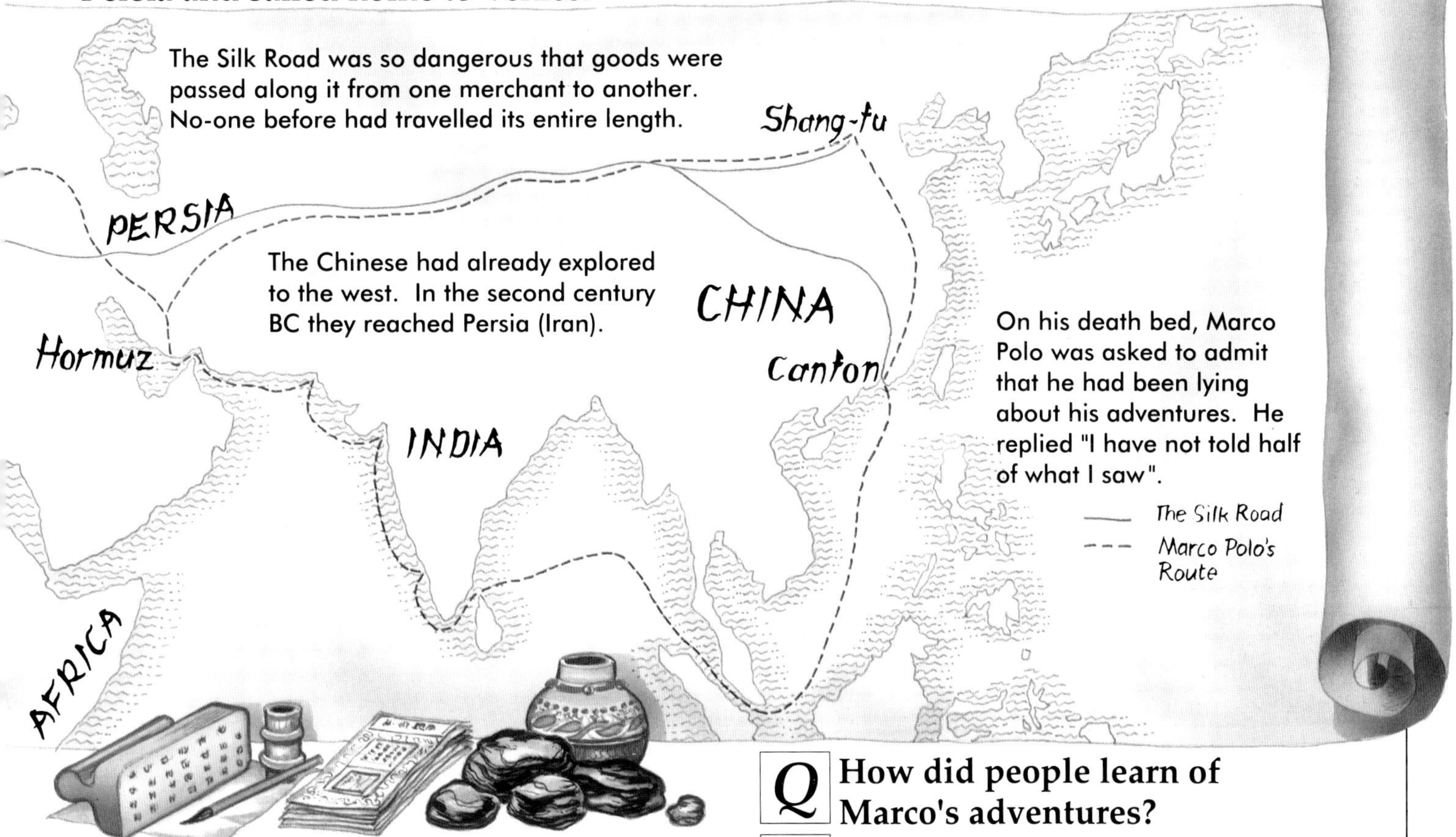

The Silk Road was so dangerous that goods were passed along it from one merchant to another. No-one before had travelled its entire length.

Shang-tu

PERSIA

The Chinese had already explored to the west. In the second century BC they reached Persia (Iran).

CHINA

Hormuz

Canton

INDIA

AFRICA

On his death bed, Marco Polo was asked to admit that he had been lying about his adventures. He replied "I have not told half of what I saw".

—— The Silk Road

- - - Marco Polo's Route

Q What new sights did Marco see?

A On his travels Marco saw many strange and wonderful things unknown to Europeans. He marvelled at the huge cities and strange-shaped ships on the great rivers. He saw, for the first time, people using paper money, burning coal not wood, and printing words on paper using wooden blocks. Marco also found sources of jewels and spices.

Q How did people learn of Marco's adventures?

A After Marco's return in 1295, war broke out between the Venetians and the Genoese, and he was taken prisoner. In prison he dictated his story to another prisoner. Many people did not believe his book, which described the discovery of oil, coal, magnificent palaces, parades of elephants, gifts to Kublai Khan of 100,000 white horses and huge jewels that were beyond the imagination of the Venetians.

When was the Great Age of Exploration?

The 15th and early 16th centuries are often called the Great Age of Exploration because so many discoveries were made at this time. Sea routes were found to the East, and unknown lands were explored - for example, America, the West Indies and the Pacific.

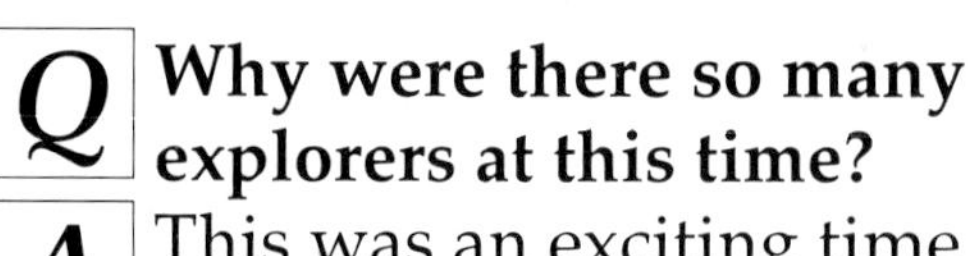

Q Why were there so many explorers at this time?

A This was an exciting time of new learning. Western Europeans wanted to find out more about the world, and had developed ships that would allow them to do so. Merchants wanted to obtain such valuable things as spices, silk, gems and fine china. Spices from the East were needed for cooking and medicines.

Q Which country began the Great Age of Exploration?

A The Portugese, in the early 15th century. Ships sailing out of Lisbon port picked up strong winds which drove them directly south until they picked up a wind to drive them east.

Q Who first sailed round the southern tip of Africa?

A The Portuguese captain, Bartolomeo Dias, in 1487. He had two caravels and a larger ship to carry stores. He sailed round the Cape of Good Hope but his crew refused to go any further.

Q Who paid for the expeditions?

A Usually they were sponsored by the royal family of a country. Prince Henry of Portugal became known as Henry the Navigator not because he ever went to sea, but because he sponsored Portuguese expeditions. Spanish and English kings and queens also paid for explorers' voyages. They wanted to find riches overseas and to gain power over any new lands that were discovered.

Q Which European first reached India by sea?

A The Portuguese sailor, Vasco da Gama. He followed Dias' route round Africa. Then he took on board an Arab pilot who helped him navigate to India. Da Gama lost two ships and half his men, but took back to Portugal a cargo of spices and precious gems.

Many of Da Gama's men died of scurvy from not having enough fresh food.

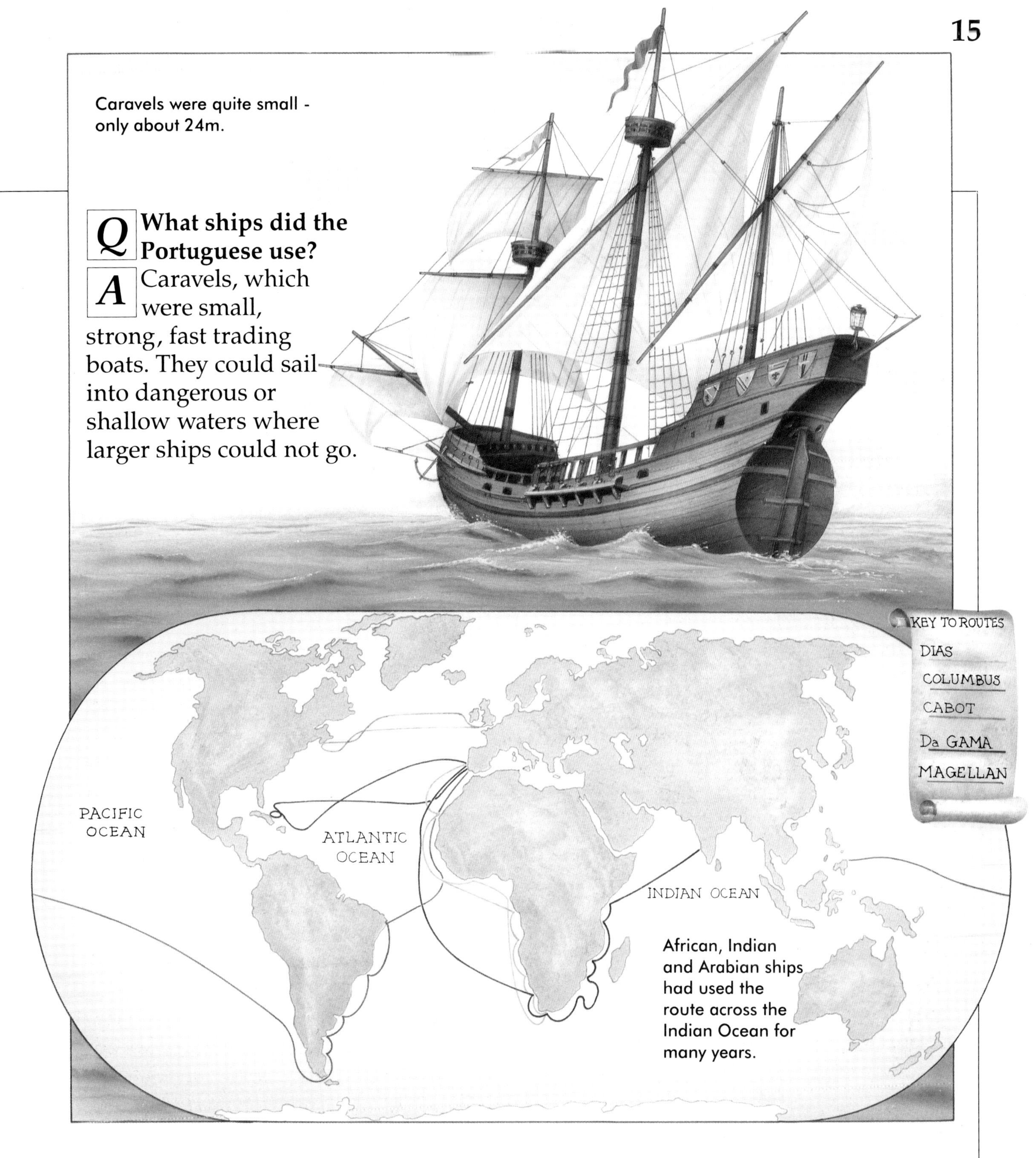

Caravels were quite small - only about 24m.

Q What ships did the Portuguese use?

A Caravels, which were small, strong, fast trading boats. They could sail into dangerous or shallow waters where larger ships could not go.

African, Indian and Arabian ships had used the route across the Indian Ocean for many years.

Q Which were the most exciting years of the Great Age of Exploration?

A These major discoveries were made within the astonishingly short space of 34 years:

1487 Dias sailed round the tip of Africa.
1492 Columbus reached the West Indies.
1497 The English explorer John Cabot reached Newfoundland, off North America.
1498 Da Gama reached India by sea.
1519-21 Magellan sailed into the Pacific.

Who discovered America?

In 1492 Christopher Columbus sailed from Spain across the Atlantic to the West Indies and found a 'New World' that nobody in Europe knew about. But people had been living in America for thousands of years before Europeans arrived.

Q Was Columbus the first European to sail to America?

A No. The Vikings had probably reached America in AD 985, but their voyages had been long forgotten when Columbus sailed.

Q How many ships did Columbus take with him?

A Columbus took three ships on his first voyage - the *Santa Maria* (his flagship), the *Nina* and the *Pinta*.

Columbus was a brave man. Da Gama knew that India existed, though he was not sure how to reach it. Columbus was sailing into the unknown.

The Santa Maria hit a coral reef in the West Indies, so only two ships made it back to Spain.

Columbus found pearls in the West Indies which made him believe he had reached China as Marco Polo's book had mentioned the Chinese diving for them.

Q Where did Columbus believe he was going?

A He thought he was going to China. When he got to the West Indies he insisted they were islands off China.

Q What did Columbus expect to find?

A He expected to find gold, pearls and spices because they were all mentioned in Marco Polo's book on China.

Q Why were Columbus's crews frightened on the voyage?

A They thought they were going too far from home and that in the Atlantic no wind ever blew in the direction of Spain, so they might never return!

Q Where does the name 'America' come from?

A It comes from Amerigo Vespucci, an Italian adventurer, who claimed that he reached the mainland of America in 1497, but it is doubtful that he did so.

Q Did Columbus actually set foot in America?

A No. He first landed in the West Indies. Later, he made three more voyages to the West Indies. On his third voyage he reached Panama, in Central America, but he never landed on the mainland of North America.

Columbus believed the world was round, so you could reach the East by sailing west. His mistake was to think the world was smaller than it is. He thought the distance from Europe to Asia was 5713km. In fact it is 18,935km.

SPAIN
Palos
AFRICA

Each day Columbus lied to his men about the distance they had travelled because they were afraid of sailing too far from Spain.

Who first sailed around the world?

Ferdinand Magellan set out from Portugal in 1519, sailing westwards (like Columbus) to try to reach the East. He sailed down the coast of South America and round into the vast ocean which he named the Pacific.

Q Why didn't Magellan tell his men where they were going?

A He thought they would be too frightened to obey him. Many sailors were afraid of sea monsters.

Q How long were Magellan's men in the Pacific without fresh food?

A They spent three months and twenty days eating biscuits full of grubs and drinking stinking water. They also ate rats to survive..

Ferdinand Magellan

Many sailors died of hunger and disease because they did not have fresh food supplies.

Q How was the passage to the Pacific discovered?

A Two of Magellan's ships were blown in a storm towards the South American coast. Just in time the crews spotted a small opening. It was the strait (passage) they were looking for. It is now called the Strait of Magellan.

Q Did Magellan actually sail round the world?

A No, he was killed in a battle with islanders in the Philippines.

Q Who led the second voyage round the world?

A Sir Francis Drake, who left Britain in 1577 to rob Spanish treasure ships. Following Magellan's route round South America, he returned to England in 1580.

Sir Francis Drake

Q How many men returned safely?

A Of the 260 or so crew aboard five ships who set out, only 18 men and one ship, the *Vittoria*, returned to Spain in 1522. They were the first people to sail right round the world.

Q What 'strange' creatures did they see?

A In St Julian Bay, South America, Magellan's men described seeing strange birds, seawolves with webbed paws at their sides, and camels without humps. These were probably puffins, seals and llamas.

Who were the 'Conquistadors'?

Spaniards were appalled by the idol worship and human sacrifice they found in Mexico and Peru.

Once Columbus had successfully sailed across the Atlantic, Spaniards began to explore Central America. Adventurers came to the Americas to make their fortunes. These men became known as *Conquistadors* (which is Spanish for conquerors).

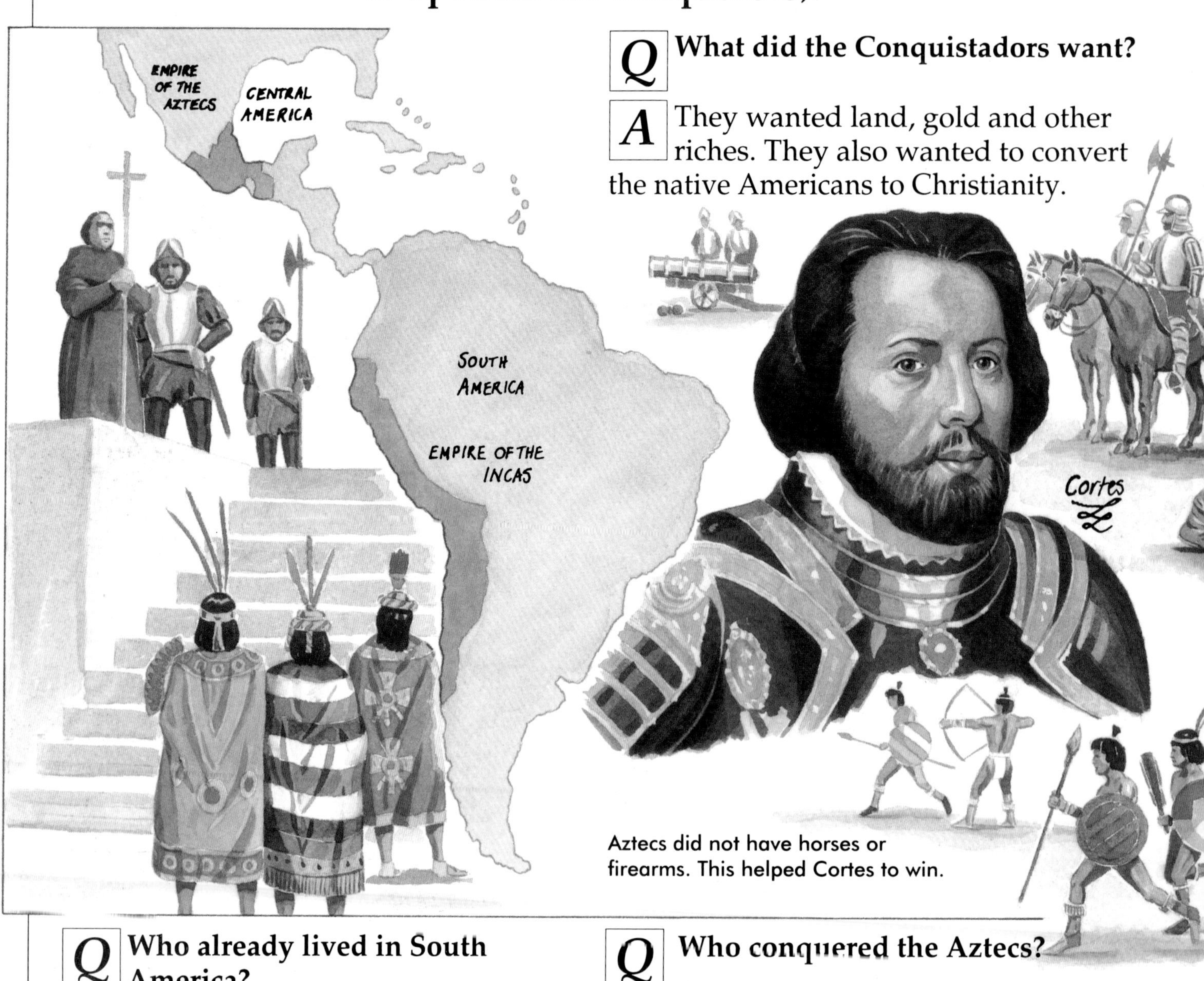

Q What did the Conquistadors want?

A They wanted land, gold and other riches. They also wanted to convert the native Americans to Christianity.

Aztecs did not have horses or firearms. This helped Cortes to win.

Q Who already lived in South America?

A Many native peoples, including the Aztecs, who ruled in Mexico, and the Incas who ruled in Peru.

Q Who conquered the Aztecs?

A The Spaniard, Hernando Cortes, landed in Mexico in 1519 with 600 soldiers and 16 horses.

Aztecs thought one of their gods, Quetzalcoatl, had a white face and black beard - like Cortes. They believed he wore a feathered head-dress, and Cortes wore a feather in his helmet.

Spaniards took cows, horses and pigs to South America.

Q How did Cortes win with so few men?

A The Aztec emperor, Montezuma, thought that Cortes might be a god and so did not fight. Later, other tribes who did not like the Aztecs helped Cortes.

Q What happened to the Incas?

A Another Spaniard, Francisco Pizarro, defeated the Incas in 1531-33 with a small army. He captured their king, said he would release him in return for a roomful of gold, then murdered the king anyway.

Thousands of Aztecs died of European diseases that the Spanish brought with them, such as smallpox, measles and colds.

When Drake returned to England in 1586, he brought news of tobacco, the Spanish name for a herb the Indians smoked.

Q What happened to the Aztecs?

A The Spaniards made the Aztecs slaves. They forced them to work hard in mines and on the land. Many died and within a few years the Aztec culture was destroyed.

Q What new items came to Europe from the New World?

A Tomatoes, chocolate (from the cacao bean) and red peppers came from America, as well as tobacco, potatoes and turkeys.

Who found out about Australia?

For a long time, geographers thought that there must be a southern continent to balance the weight of Europe and Asia, north of the Equator. They called this land Terra Australis Nondum Cognita (southern land not yet known).

Cook thought kangaroos looked like dogs, except that they jumped like hares.

Q Who first reached Australia?

A Aboriginal peoples have been living in Australia for thousands of years. The first European to sail there was a Dutch explorer, Willem Jansz, who reached the northern tip of Australia in 1606. Soon after, other Dutch ships explored the south seas, including, in 1642, Abel Tasman. He discovered Tasmania and went on to reach New Zealand.

Q Which explorers first saw kangaroos?

A Cook's crew saw kangaroos when the *Endeavour* ran aground off eastern Australia and took seven weeks to repair.

On long voyages, sailors usually got scurvy because they ate little fresh food and few vegetables. Cook made sure his men ate healthily.

Q Who first landed on the east coast of Australia?

A Captain James Cook landed in 1770. The British Admiralty had sent him on a voyage of exploration.

When Flinders got back, his ship was so rotten he could push a stick right through the bottom timbers.

Q Who first sailed right round Australia?

A A British naval officer, Matthew Flinders, between 1801 and 1803. He discovered how big Australia is, but his crew caught scurvy and his own health was damaged.

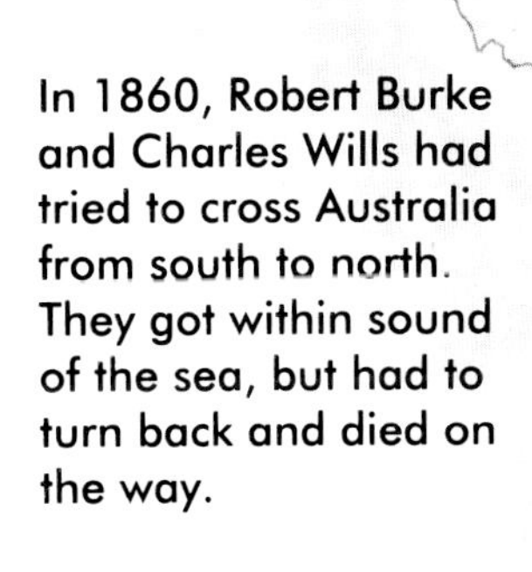

In 1860, Robert Burke and Charles Wills had tried to cross Australia from south to north. They got within sound of the sea, but had to turn back and died on the way.

Q Who first crossed Australia from south to north?

A John Stuart, a Scotsman, crossed from Adelaide to Darwin in 1862. As a reward, he won a prize of £10,000 offered by the Australian government.

Stuart was so exhausted he had to be carried back in a sling tied between two horses.

Q Why did early settlers in the east keep to the coastal areas?

A They could not find a way over the Blue Mountains, west of Sydney. In 1813, John Blaxland, William Lawson and William Wentworth got through by climbing the mountain ridges instead of following the valleys.

Q How did the explorers treat the Aborigines?

A They assumed Europeans were superior and so had a right to take the Aborigines' land. The Aboriginal lifestyle was soon almost destroyed.

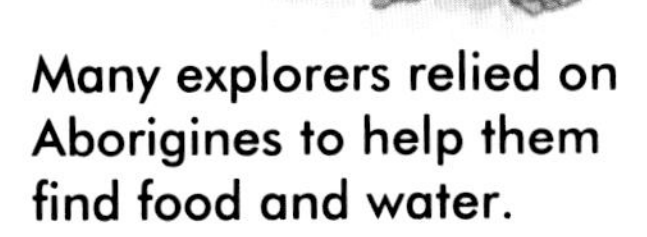

Many explorers relied on Aborigines to help them find food and water.

Who explored Africa?

Explorers faced fierce animals and dangerous conditions.

Africa is a huge continent that was first explored by Europeans in the 19th century. Its deserts, rivers, plains and jungles were uncharted, making journeys difficult and dangerous.

Q Why was Africa so dangerous for explorers?

A Africa was such a wild place that it took very determined explorers to brave the hazards. They had to put up with disease, fierce animals, rugged surroundings and often hostile people.

Livingstone was once attacked by a lion, he survived but was badly injured.

Q Who was the greatest explorer in Africa?

A The British explorer and missionary (spreader of Christianity) David Livingstone travelled nearly 50,000km through Africa from 1841 until his death in 1873. He went missing in 1866 and was not found again until 1871. He was found by the American explorer Henry Morton Stanley who used the famous greeting: "Doctor Livingstone, I presume?"

Q Who found the source of the River Nile?

A The River Nile is the longest river in the world. It flows for 6650km through North Africa to the Mediterranean Sea. John Hanning Speke, a British explorer, discovered in 1862 that the Nile flowed out of Lake Victoria.

The highest African mountain is Kilimanjaro (5895m) in Tanzania. A German, Hans Meyer, first reached the highest peak in 1889.

Q Who was the most famous woman explorer of Africa?

A In the 1890s a British woman, Mary Kingsley, explored West Africa and discovered many unknown species of birds and animals. She also fought for justice and medical care for the African people.

Q Who explored the Sahara Desert?

A The Sahara is the largest desert in the world with an area of 9 million sq km. One third of it is sand and the rest rocky wasteland. In the 1820s the Scottish explorers Hugh Clapperton and Walter Oudney, and English soldier Dixon Denham crossed the Sahara and made friends with Arab leaders.

Q What other great discoveries were made in Africa?

A The German explorer Heinrich Barth discovered the source of the River Niger in the 1850s and also discovered a new route across the Sahara Desert.

How were polar regions explored?

On his journey to the North Pole, Robert Peary learned much from the Inuit (Eskimos) in his party.

The polar regions were only fully explored in the 20th century. Polar exploration is still difficult today but modern technology has made the task less hazardous.

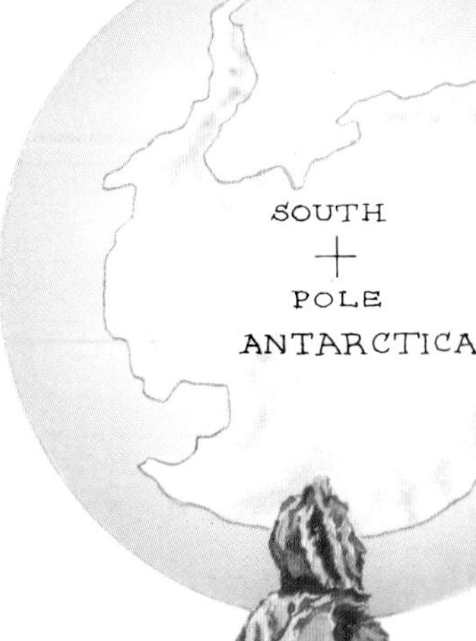

Q What are the differences between the North and the South Poles?

A The North Pole is in the frozen Arctic Ocean, which is surrounded by inhabited lands such as Greenland, Alaska and Canada. The South Pole is in Antarctica, which is a vast uninhabited area of frozen land surrounded by sea.

Q Who first reached the North Pole?

A In 1909 an American naval officer, Robert Peary, and his team, reached the North Pole with supplies pulled by a team of huskies. He suffered severe frostbite and lost all his toes.

Q Who first reached the South Pole?

A In 1911 the Norwegian Roald Amundsen reached the South Pole just one month ahead of the British naval officer Robert Falcon Scott, who reached the Pole in January 1912. Scott and his four companions died during their return trip.

Q How did Amundsen beat Scott to the South Pole?

A Amundsen used dog teams (huskies) while Scott had ponies which could not stand the cold. Scott and his men ended up pulling their sledges themselves.

The boots of early polar explorers were sometimes stuffed with grass to keep their feet warm!

Q What did early polar explorers wear?

A Scott's team wore clothes made of cotton and wool which absorbed sweat, making them cold and wet. Amundsen's men wore furs and animal skins which let the body breathe as well as keeping it warm.

Q How do polar explorers keep warm today?

A They wear layers of clothes, trapping air between them. One layer is waterproof to stop sweat soaking outer layers of clothing. Outer clothes are windproof and padded.

Q What kind of shelters are needed?

A Tents are still used today but they are better insulated against the weather than those of the early explorers. Scientists working in polar regions for months at a time have proper buildings to work in.

Q What are the main dangers faced by polar explorers?

A Exposure (when the body is so chilled it cannot function) is the most serious hazard in polar cold. Frostbite, when the circulation of blood stops in fingers and toes, is another. Well-insulated clothes and warm food keep these at bay.

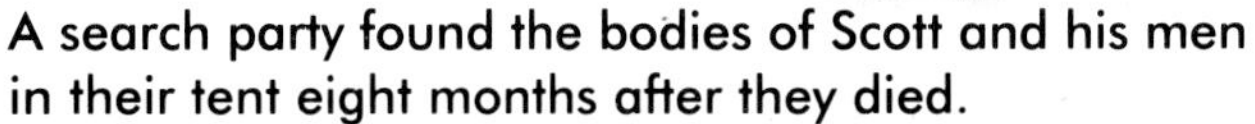

A search party found the bodies of Scott and his men in their tent eight months after they died.

In Halley's diving bell of 1717, fresh air was supplied from a barrel.

How is the sea explored?

Water pressure increases with depth. Divers working for long periods deep under the sea can suffer burst eardrums and internal bleeding.

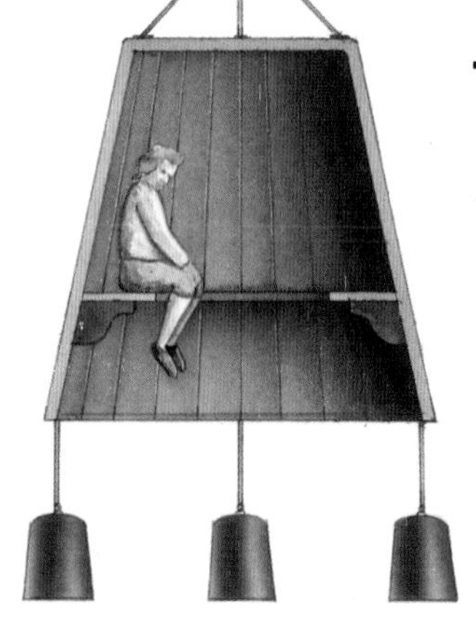

Underwater exploration reveals a strange and beautiful world. There are undersea mountains higher than any on the surface of the Earth, and millions of sea creatures. On the sea bed there are many ancient shipwrecks.

Q Why explore the sea bed?

A Scientists want to discover more about the Earth's structure and life on the sea bed. There are also valuable minerals, such as oil, under the sea. Some explorers are interested in shipwrecks and the cargo they carried.

Q How can people explore great depths?

A Special underwater craft have been designed. For example, Frenchman Auguste Piccard and his son Jacques designed a deep-diving craft called a bathyscaphe. In 1960 Jacques took the bathyscaphe *Trieste* down to a depth of 11km under the Pacific Ocean. It took five hours to reach the sea bed. There are also small submarines, called submersibles, that can dive as deep as 6000m.

Q What is a diving bell?

A It is an early underwater exploration device. Air from the surface was pumped into a bell-shaped container. A diver could sit inside it and explore under the sea, but could not go very deep.

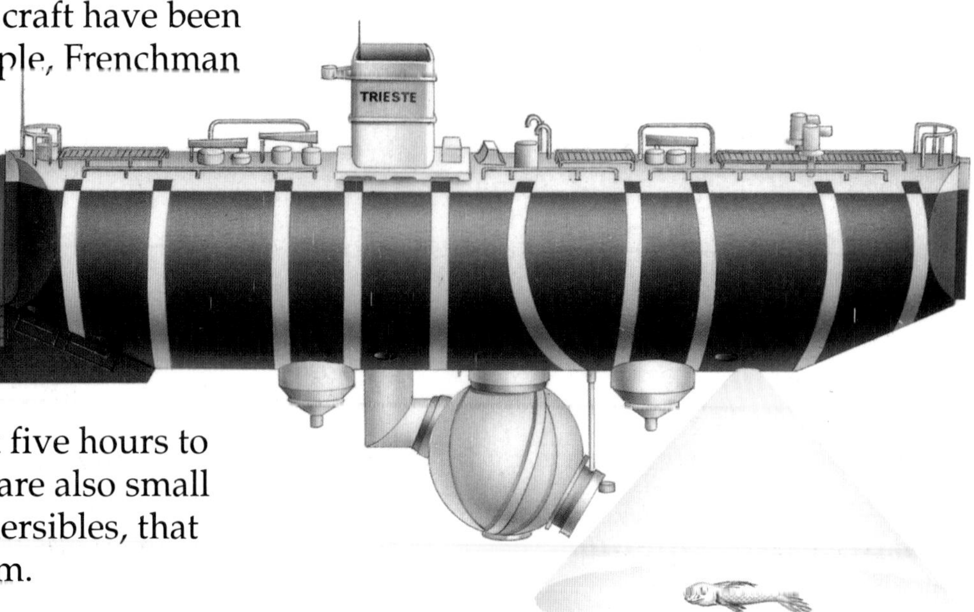

In the deepest parts of the oceans it is very cold and there is no light. Even so, some creatures are found living there.

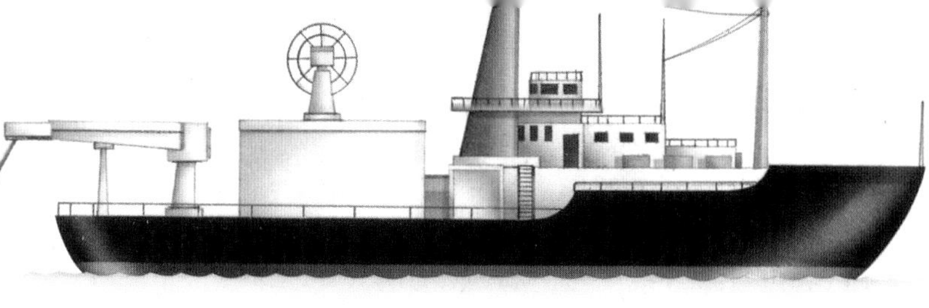

Submersibles work from and return to a 'mother ship' on the surface.

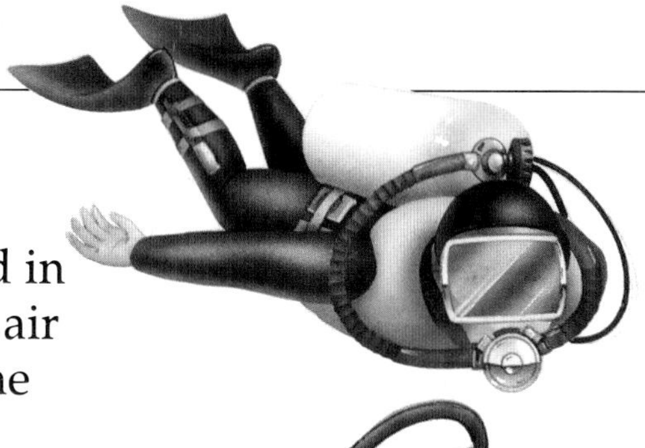

Q What is an aqualung?

A It is an underwater breathing device invented in 1943 by the French. Cylinders of compressed air are fastened to the diver's back and a tube feeds the air to a mouthpiece. With this, divers can safely descend to a depth of about 73m, carrying their air supply with them.

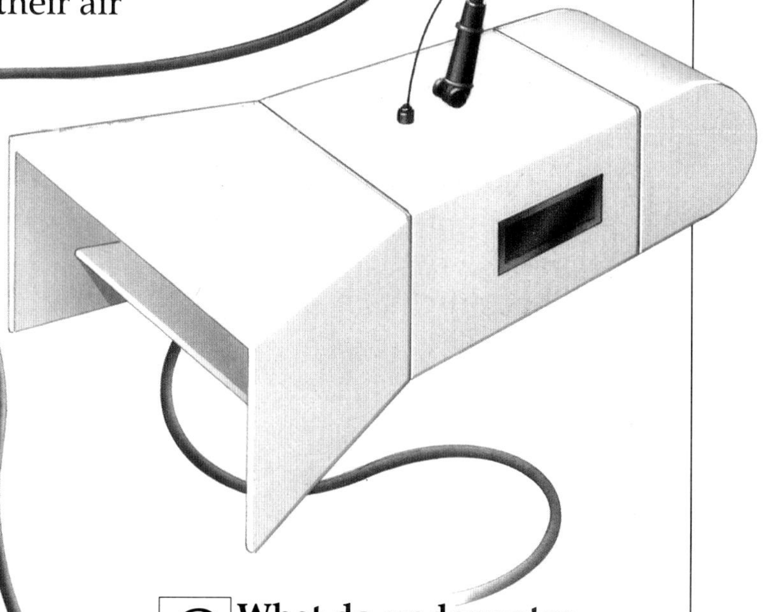

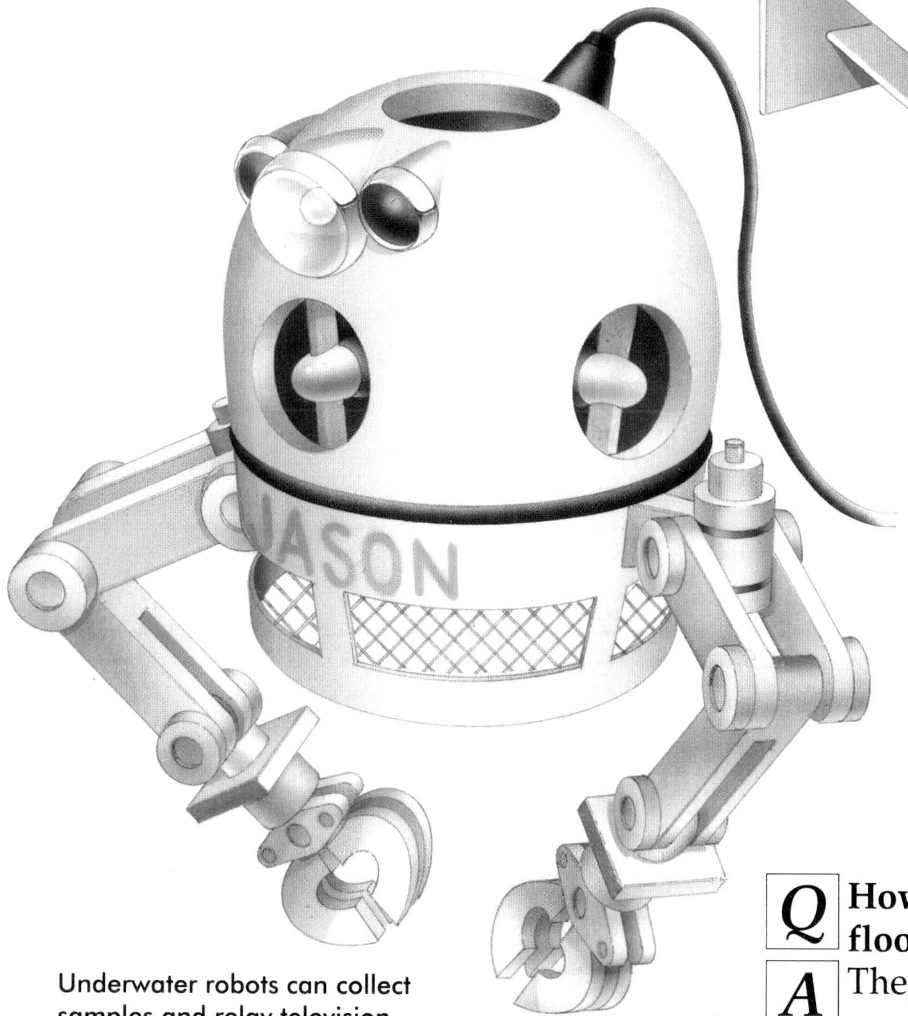

Q What do underwater robots do?

A Underwater search robots have been developed. They were used to explore the sunken remains of ships such as the *Titanic* and the *Bismark*. The robots are controlled from the surface, so human lives are not put at risk.

Q How do scientists map the sea floor?

A They use echo-sounding equipment to chart the shape of the sea bed. This works like radar, bouncing sound waves off objects.

Underwater robots can collect samples and relay television pictures to the surface.

How is space explored?

The Russian word for astronaut is 'cosmonaut'. In 1963 the first woman in space was cosmonaut Valentina Tereshkova.

Space explorers use shuttles and robot craft to investigate the solar system and beyond. Scientists learn more every day about planets and stars through the pictures and information sent back to earth.

Q When was the first rocket invented?

A The Chinese invented gunpowder which they used to fire the first rockets in 1232.

Q Who was the first person to travel in a rocket?

A An un-named woman pilot during the Second World War (1939-45) tested a German rocket that was capable of travelling long distances.

Q Who was the first person in space?

A The first person to leave the Earth's atmosphere in a rocket was a Russian, Yuri Gagarin. He made one orbit of Earth on 12 April 1961, in Vostok 1. The flight lasted 1 hour and 48 minutes.

Q What is a space shuttle?

A A shuttle is a vehicle sent into space attached to a rocket. After leaving the rocket it is used to complete tasks in space, such as launching satellites. Then the shuttle is flown back to Earth to be used again.

Space shuttles land on a runway just like large gliders.

Astronauts talk to each other by radio as in space there are no air waves to carry sound.

The first person to walk on the Moon was American astronaut Neil Armstrong on 20 July 1969.

Astronauts have to strap themselves into chairs because there is no gravity in a spacecraft and they would float around inside.

Q How are astronauts able to leave a spacecraft?

A To travel outside their spacecraft, astronauts wear special sealed suits equipped with oxygen. They may also be linked to the spaceship by a lifeline. A jet booster pack helps them move around.

Q What do astronauts eat?

A Food on board a spacecraft is mostly dried then rehydrated before eating. It can be eaten with a spoon and fork or sucked through a tube.

Q What are space probes?

A They are unmanned robot spacecraft that explore deep into space for years and transmit information back to Earth. A probe cannot usually return to Earth.

Astronauts do not use a normal toilet. Waste is sucked into bags for disposal back on Earth.

Index